LOTS OF THINGS TO KNOW ABOUT
OUR WORLD

James Maclaine

Illustrated by
Malgorzata Detner

Designed by
Lenka Jones and Meg Tall

With expert advice from Dr. Roger Trend

USBORNE QUICKLINKS

Scan the code for links to websites with amazing videos, activities and facts about our world, or go to **usborne.com/Quicklinks** and type in the title of this book.

You can also download a map of the world at Usborne Quicklinks if you want to find any of the places mentioned on the following pages.

Usborne Publishing is not responsible for the content of external websites. Children should be supervised online. Please follow the online safety guidelines at **usborne.com/Quicklinks**

TRIPS AROUND THE WORLD

"Which continent would you like to visit first?"

"I'm not sure. What is a CONTINENT?"

"You can check the meaning of that word in the glossary on page 62. And there's an index on pages 63-64 to help you search for a topic."

Spinning world

Have you ever played with a globe?
It's a 3D model of our world — **Planet Earth**.

When you push on a globe to make it spin, you see the way that Earth — and everything on it — spins around and around in space.

Planet Earth always turns in the same direction. It takes 24 hours to do a full spin.

> Like this torch, the Sun lights up one side of the world, while the other side is in darkness.

As the planet spins, day fades to night. That's why people on the other side of the world from you might be fast asleep as you read this.

Five oceans...

There are five **oceans** in the world. Imagine pouring all the water in each one into five enormous jars...

Look at the size of these jars to see how the amounts of water in the oceans compare.

The Arctic Ocean would fill the smallest jar.

Save the VERY BIGGEST jar for the Pacific.

Scientists have worked out that it contains as much water as the other four combined.

I feel thirsty looking at all this water.

You can't drink one drop. It's all salty seawater.

...and seven continents

The land in the world can be divided into seven **continents**. To compare how much each continent covers, check the size of these plates...

The BIGGEST continent, Asia, is also home to the MOST people.

Even though it's bigger than Europe and Oceania, hardly anyone lives in Antarctica. Only a few thousand scientists stay there each year.

So MANY people

Long ago, there were far, far, far fewer people in the world than there are now.

The total number grew slowly for thousands of years. Then, in 1804, there was some amazing news...

HURRAH! PLANET EARTH IS HOME TO ONE BILLION PEOPLE (FOR THE FIRST TIME)

1804

How do I write one billion in numbers?

1,000,000,000 – that's one 1 followed by nine 0s.

TWO BILLION HUMANS IN THE WORLD

1927

The number kept on growing... By 1927, it had DOUBLED.

What's inside the Earth?

If you could slice Planet Earth in half, you'd be able to count different layers inside.

One, two, three... FOUR LAYERS!

The top layer is called the **crust**. It's made of rock.

All the land is part of the crust...

...and it holds all the oceans, too.

CRUST

MANTLE

Below the crust is the thickest layer: the **mantle**. It's mostly solid rock, but it's hotter than the crust, so some parts are melted.

Scientists think that there could be enough GOLD in the outer core and inner core to coat the surface of the entire planet.

OUTER CORE

The third layer down is liquid. Called the **outer core**, it's made of iron, nickel, gold and other types of metals. The metals are melted because it's so hot.

INNER CORE

Lastly, the **inner core** is in the middle. It's even hotter, but the metals here are kept solid and don't melt. That's because of the enormous weight of all the layers above.

The capital city with the longest name

Almost every country has one chief city, known as its **capital**.

Thailand's capital city is called Bangkok. Much longer is its full name in the Thai language. If you wanted to write out all 168 letters on an envelope, it would need to be a big one...

Krungthepmahanakhonamon-
rattanakosinmahintharaayu-
thayamahadilokphopnop-
pharatratchathaniburiromu-
domratchaniwetmahasathan-
amonpimanawatansathitsak-
kathattiyawitsanukamprasit

And that's ONLY the name of the city!

Bolivia has TWO CAPITALS – La Paz and Sucre. South Africa has THREE – Pretoria, Cape Town and Bloemfontein.

One-letter places

In Norway and Sweden, there are several villages that are surprisingly easy to spell. They all have the same name that's made up of one letter only — Å.

Å is an extra letter in the Norwegian and Swedish alphabets.

It has a little circle at the top.

Å is also an old word for a small river.

How do you say Å?

It sounds like the O in the word MORE.

The greatest light shows on Earth

Looking up at the night sky, you might expect to see stars and the Moon. But in some parts of the world, you might be lucky enough to spot SPECTACULAR displays of lights.

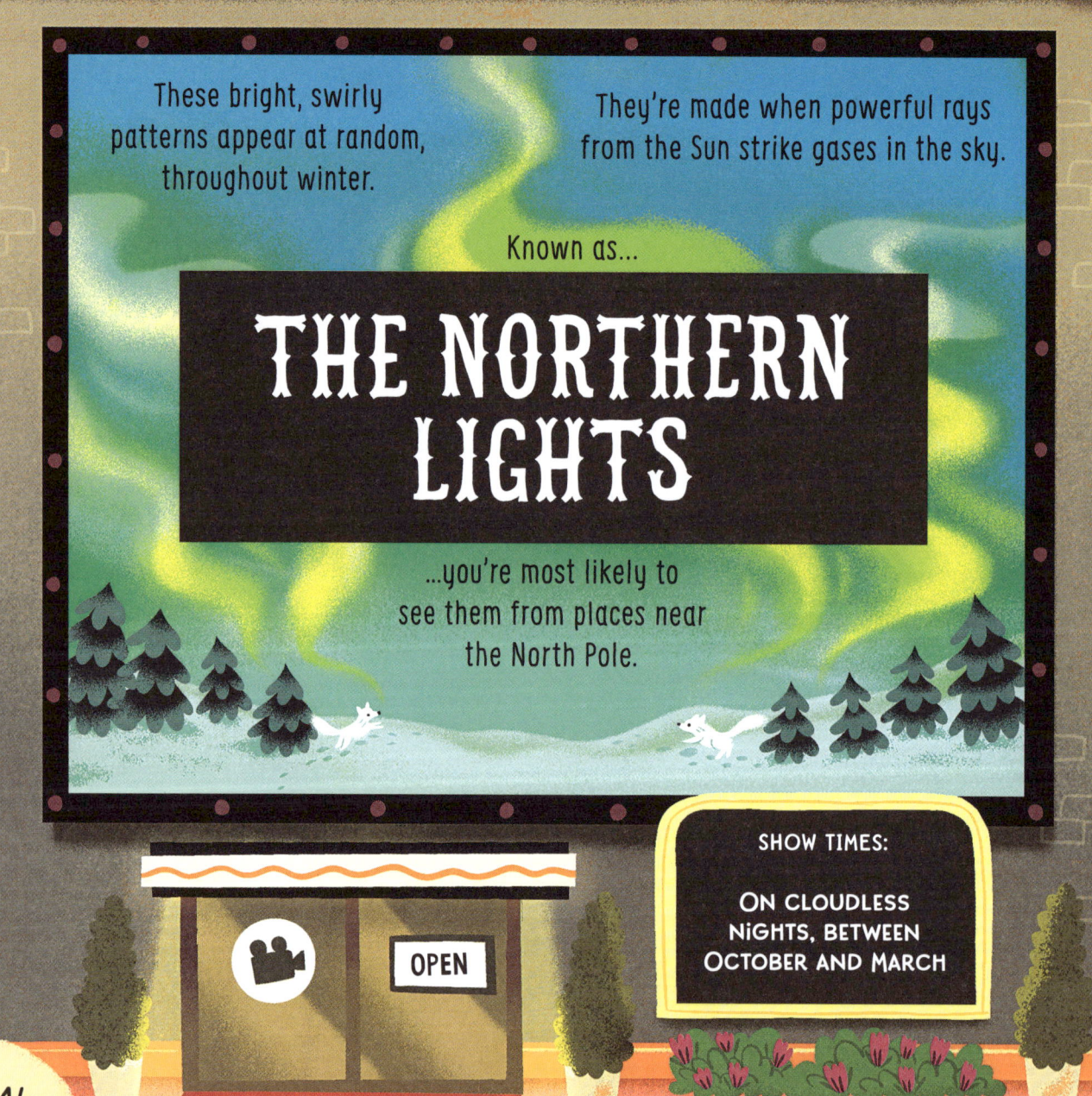

These bright, swirly patterns appear at random, throughout winter.

They're made when powerful rays from the Sun strike gases in the sky.

Known as...

THE NORTHERN LIGHTS

...you're most likely to see them from places near the North Pole.

SHOW TIMES:

ON CLOUDLESS NIGHTS, BETWEEN OCTOBER AND MARCH

If you're somewhere close to the South Pole, you might still see lights just as pretty. They have a different name:

THE SOUTHERN LIGHTS

The displays can last a few minutes, or, sometimes, an hour or two.

SHOW TIMES:

ON CLOUDLESS NIGHTS, BETWEEN MAY AND AUGUST

When it's winter in the south, it's summer in the north.

I guess you have to be in the right place at the right time to see the lights.

15

Flag shapes

Every country has its own **flag**. And almost all of them are rectangular.

The Danish flag is one of the **oldest**. It's been flown for over 600 years.

Just two countries have square-shaped flags.

Vatican City is the SMALLEST COUNTRY in the world. It's inside the Italian city of Rome.

This is the only flag that has five sides. It's made up of two triangles, joined together.

Country songs

Every country has a **national anthem**. It's a song that people who live there sing on important occasions. Sometimes, fans sing these anthems when supporting their country's sports teams.

O Canada...

GO TEAM CANADA

O Canada...

O Canada...

It's a little trickier for the people of Kosovo, Bosnia and Herzegovina, San Marino and Spain. Their national anthems don't have any words.

Hhmmm...

VAMOS ESPANA

Hhmmm...

Have Spain's fans forgotten what to sing?

No! They're doing their best humming.

The changing faces of Planet Earth

Looking at these pictures and globes, you might think they show nine different planets. In fact, each one is Earth at a different stage of its lifetime — that's OVER 4.5 BILLION YEARS so far.

At the start, Earth was a red-hot, melted ball.

4.5 BILLION YEARS AGO

Then its surface cooled and hardened.

Rain poured for hundreds of years, making the first seas.

3.8 BILLION YEARS AGO

Later, temperatures dropped so low that sheets of ice covered the whole planet.

700 MILLION YEARS AGO

Scientists call this Snowball Earth.

300 MILLION YEARS AGO

Eventually, the ice melted. Around this time, Earth had just one giant continent.

As millions of years went by, the continent broke up into separate continents.

The continents drifted apart from each other...

150 MILLION YEARS AGO

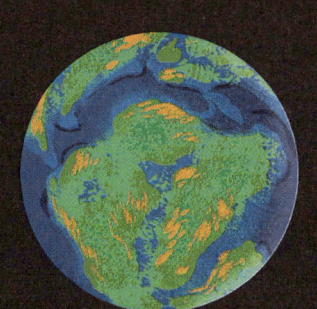

...and the oceans between them grew wider.

100 MILLION YEARS AGO

By this point, ice froze across some of the continents.

20 MILLION YEARS AGO

Nowadays, the planet's surface looks like this...

NOW

The continents are still moving. But it's happening far too slowly for you to notice.

AT NIGHT

And when it gets dark, the world starts to twinkle. That's because of all the bright lights in big cities.

I wonder what Planet Earth will look like in a million years' time...

Talking to the world

If you want to talk to everybody in the world, you'll need to learn over 7,000 languages. But you could start by finding out how to say **hello** in the 20 most spoken languages.

Merhaba TURKISH

Salut FRENCH

Halo INDONESIAN

Namaste HINDI

All the languages on these pages are used in lots of different countries.

Hola SPANISH

Ahlan wa sahlan EGYPTIAN ARABIC

Nomoskar BENGALI

> Greetings, hey, howdy, hi... Just as in English, there are other words for saying hello in each language.

Olá PORTUGUESE

Marhaba STANDARD ARABIC

20

Hello — ENGLISH

More than a billion people speak English and more than a billion people speak Mandarin Chinese.

Ni hao — MANDARIN CHINESE

Many, many millions of people speak each of the other 18 languages.

Konnichiwa — JAPANESE

How far? — NIGERIAN PIDGIN

All together, the speakers of these 20 languages make up almost half the planet.

Assalam-u-alikum — URDU

Hallo — GERMAN

Sannu — HAUSA

Namaskar — MARATHI

Vanakkam — TAMIL

Privet — RUSSIAN

Halo — TELUGU

How many of the languages had you heard of before?

The grand forest tour

Visit some of the world's forests to see trees that soar up to the clouds and to hear the sounds of sometimes unknown animals.

Boreal forests in northern parts of the planet look wintry for more than half the year.

The trees have chemicals in their leaves to stop them freezing.

Bamboo plants are grasses, but they can grow as tall as trees.

Bamboo forests in China are good for pandas to hide in – and to eat.

Trees to rival skyscrapers!

The tallest trees are **coast redwoods**. They tower above forests along North America's west coast.

Taller than the tallest?

Each of these mountains has a claim to be the **tallest** in the world. Read on to find out how...

MOUNT EVEREST
BETWEEN NEPAL AND CHINA

MAUNA KEA
IN HAWAII

There's no doubt that **Mount Everest** is the highest of all the mountains above sea level.

ABOVE SEA LEVEL means from the top of the sea.

SNOW LEOPARD

But **Mauna Kea** grows up from the ocean floor. If you measured from there, you'd find it's taller than Everest.

HAWAIIAN HOARY BAT

Ah, look! Mauna Kea slopes down below the water.

Which countries grow the most food?

Browse these supermarket shelves to find out the countries where farmers produce the most of different kinds of **food** – by weight.

BLACK PEPPER
VIETNAM

DATES
EGYPT

Fruit, such as dates, and other crops need different amounts of rainfall and sunshine to grow best.

QUINOA
PERU

Cool temperatures in Peru are ideal for quinoa plants. Their seeds are delicious when cooked.

OLIVE OIL
SPAIN

Olives are squashed to make olive oil.

Lots of places in Spain have dry soil that's good for growing olives.

CHEESE
USA

Because so many people live there, China grows the most of many types of vegetables, including carrots.

CARROTS
CHINA

AVOCADOS
MEXICO

Many Mexican dishes have avocados in them. Farmers are more likely to grow things that people who live nearby eat a lot.

ORANGES
BRAZIL

COCOA
CÔTE D'IVOIRE

VANILLA
MADAGASCAR

Oooh, there's cocoa in these chocolate bars – yummy!

Vanilla plants are tricky to grow. But farmers in Madagascar know how to care for them. That's excellent news if you like vanilla ice cream.

...to the driest

Much of Antarctica is covered in ice and snow. But there's a wide-open space where the ground is stony and bone dry...

McMURDO DRY VALLEYS
THE DRIEST PLACE ON PLANET EARTH

The few times it snows, strong winds blow it all away.

No plants can grow here.

Penguins that live in Antarctica sometimes stumble into the valleys by mistake.

I don't like the look of this place.

Where's all the ice?

ADÉLIE PENGUIN

Amazing ways to get around

Forget about taking a taxi or riding a bus. Here are some places with much more memorable ways to travel.

MONTE TO FUNCHAL, MADEIRA

It might look a little like a toboggan, but this basket on wooden skids doesn't need any snow.

Two drivers push the basket...

Screeech

...and use the chunky soles of their shoes as brakes.

The drivers only go downhill. It's a one-way trip!

LA PAZ TO EL ALTO, BOLIVIA

The world's largest system of cable cars has more than 30 stations. It connects two cities.

ALONG THE OKAVANGO RIVER, BOTSWANA

Watch out for hippos from the safety of a mokoro.

This canoe-like boat glides through the reeds with the push of a pole on the riverbed.

ACROSS CHIBA, JAPAN

Do all trains move on top of tracks? Think again.

Hanging down instead, the Chiba Urban Monorail carries passengers above the city.

Where stinky flowers bloom and cloud-shaped plants grow

You'd have to visit a few particular places in the world to find these unusual plants growing wild.

Dotted across the **Andes** mountains, yaretas slowly grow into amazing cloud shapes — without any gardener pruning them.

These dainty flowers cling onto rocky places in **Gibraltar** — and nowhere else.

GIBRALTAR CAMPION

YARETA

If you go to the **Sonoran Desert**, you can see saguaros.

They sprout arms as they get older to keep more water inside them.

SAGUARO

Shape-shifting caves

Under the ground, all sorts of **caves** are slowly changing shape.

As rainwater drips through the ground above, tiny amounts of rock dissolve into it.

To see how things DISSOLVE, keep stirring some salt into warm water until it disappears.

When the drips reach the air inside the cave, the rock hardens again.

This makes spine shapes that hang down — called **stalactites**...

...and **stalagmites** that poke up.

As years go by, stalactites and stalagmites grow longer and longer. Sometimes, they join together.

Rocks for dinner?

Even weirder rocks can form in other parts of caves. Some of them have surprising names to describe the way they look.

CAVE POPCORN

Not a tasty snack! These pale, rocky clusters cling to cave walls and ledges.

SODA STRAW

This type of cave rock is as hollow as a drinking straw.

CAVE BACON

You don't need that fork – they're rocks.

Sheets of cave bacon are thin and striped — just like the slices of meat.

The Earth's shield

Every day, lots of space rocks — called **meteoroids** — hurtle towards our planet.

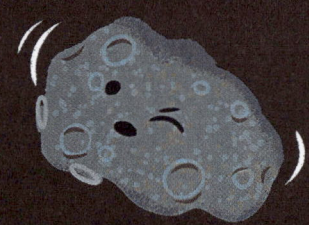

But don't worry. The Earth is surrounded and protected by layers of gases. They make up the **atmosphere**.

Uh-oh...

ATMOSPHERE

When meteoroids enter the atmosphere, they rub against the gases and BURN UP. Then they're known as **meteors**.

METEOR

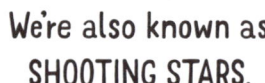

We're also known as SHOOTING STARS.

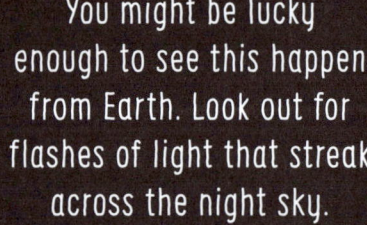

You might be lucky enough to see this happen from Earth. Look out for flashes of light that streak across the night sky.

Take that, space rock!

Ancient scars

If meteoroids make it through the atmosphere and reach Earth intact, they become **meteorites**.

When big meteorites struck the ground long ago, they left behind dents, called **craters**.

These craters are so wide and deep you can see them from high in the sky.

You can even sail a boat inside a few of them.

LAKE BOSOMTWE, GHANA

Over time, this crater filled with rainwater, making a lake.

Don't forget your sunglasses...

There's nowhere sandier than the **Sahara**. This **desert** spreads across eleven countries, covering much of northern Africa.

SUN

All that sand warms up very quickly in the blazing sunshine.

Whew! It's HOT.

Then, the sand heats up the air above it just as fast, making temperatures SOAR.

To escape the heat, desert animals hide under the ground, in their burrows.

You're better off down here, cubs. It's much cooler.

FENNEC FOX

...and don't forget your scarf

As night falls, the Sun is no longer around to heat the sand. So the sand loses all its warmth to the air.

Rain clouds and mist could keep heat in the air. But, as in all deserts, it hardly ever rains in the Sahara. The air here is extremely dry.

MOON

With no clouds or mist to hold onto the heat, the temperature gets lower and lower and lower, until it's **freezing cold**.

"BRRRR! You're going to need to wrap up warm later."

This is good news for the fennec fox. It can now go out hunting without overheating.

"My fluffy fur protects me from the chill."

The islands of GIANT tortoises

The Galápagos Islands, off the coast of South America, are home to the world's BIGGEST tortoises. As heavy as ponies, these giants are found NOWHERE else in the world.

GALÁPAGOS GIANT TORTOISE

DARWIN'S FINCH

I peck off tiny bugs that live on tortoise skin.

Thanks, finch!

The name Galápagos comes from an old Spanish word for tortoises.

There are other islands in the world that are the ONLY places where certain animals live.

MINDORO — SOUTHEAST ASIA

TAMARAW

CUBA — CARIBBEAN

I'm the SMALLEST kind of bird.

BEE HUMMINGBIRD

ACTUAL SIZE!

GRAND CAYMAN — CARIBBEAN

BLUE IGUANA

MADAGASCAR — SOUTHEAST AFRICA

AYE-AYE

How many more islands are there in the world?

MILLIONS! There are so many that no one knows the exact number.

ISLA ESCUDO DE VERAGUAS — CENTRAL AMERICA

PYGMY SLOTH

Quakeproof buildings

When **earthquakes** happen, the ground can shake for a few seconds or minutes. Many buildings around the world are designed to withstand the shaking...

FA-BO BUILDING, JAPAN

A web of rods around this office supports the walls and keeps them stable.

TORRE REFORMA, MEXICO

Most of the time, earthquakes are so gentle that nobody notices them.

Phew!

This skyscraper's walls extend far underground to give it extra support.

BAMBOO HOUSES, LOMBOK

Built from the flexible stems of bamboo plants, these houses can wobble safely without breaking.

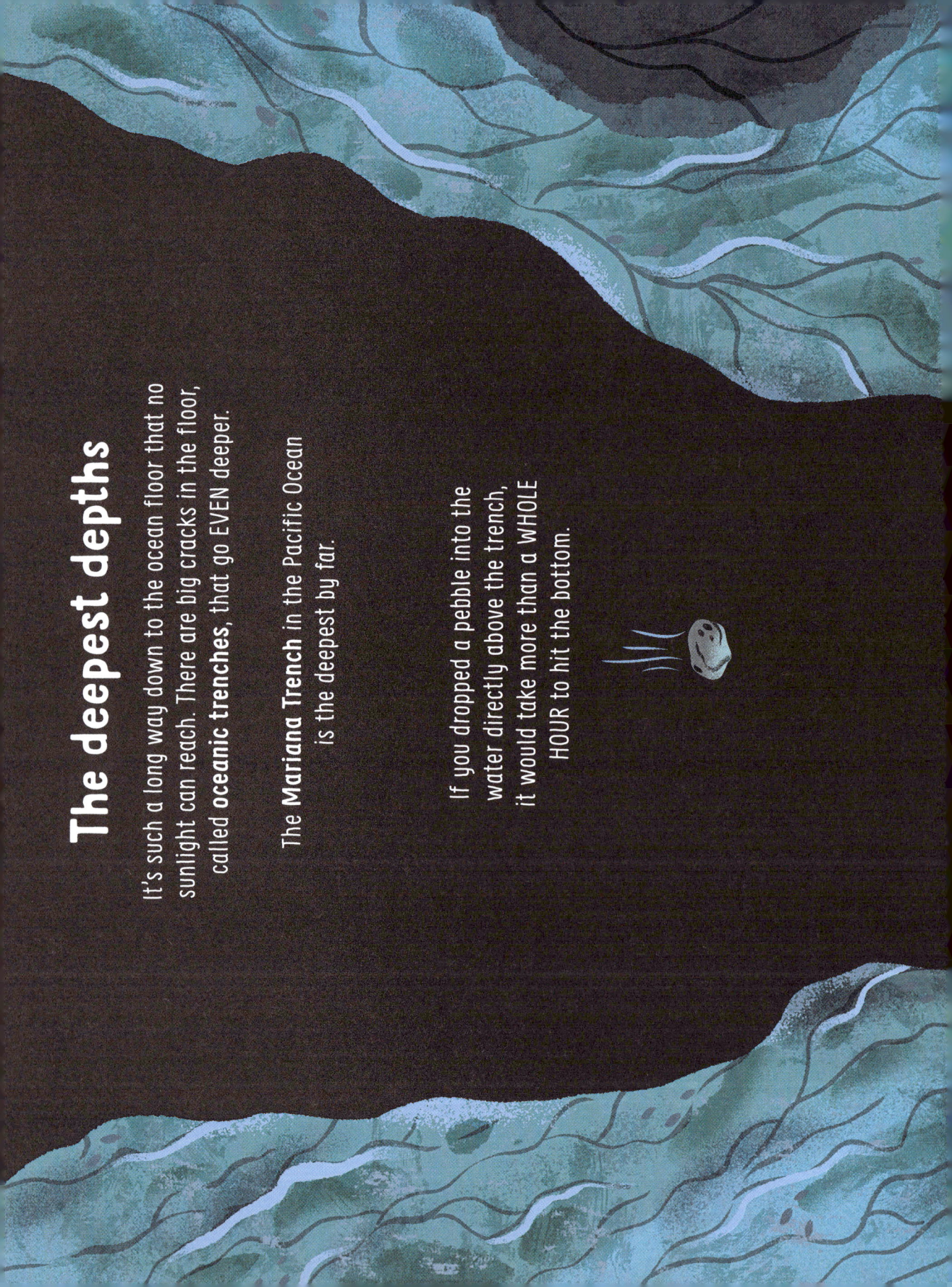

The deepest depths

It's such a long way down to the ocean floor that no sunlight can reach. There are big cracks in the floor, called **oceanic trenches**, that go EVEN deeper.

The **Mariana Trench** in the Pacific Ocean is the deepest by far.

If you dropped a pebble into the water directly above the trench, it would take more than a WHOLE HOUR to hit the bottom.

Record-breaking sights

If you set off to see some of the world's tallest, biggest and oldest sights, you could bring back postcards and stickers as souvenirs.

The Statue of Unity in Gujarat, India, is the world's **tallest statue**.

It's more than three times taller than the Statue of Liberty in New York, USA.

STATUE OF LIBERTY

STATUE OF UNITY

Wish you were here...

RIDEAU CANAL

The **biggest pineapple-shaped building** is in Bathurst, South Africa. It's called the Big Pineapple — of course.

Each winter, the Rideau Canal in Ottawa, Canada, freezes over to make the **largest skating rink**.

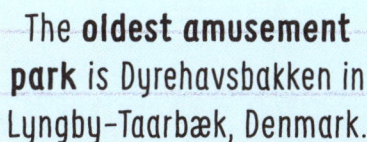

The **oldest amusement park** is Dyrehavsbakken in Lyngby-Taarbæk, Denmark.

The **longest staircase** goes up the Niesen mountain in Switzerland. To climb up it, you'll have to ready yourself for 11,674 steps.

To see the painting on this postcard, you'll have to go to the Louvre, in Paris, France. It's the **most visited museum**.

Built over 4,500 years ago, the Great Pyramid of Giza, Egypt, is still the **tallest pyramid**.

Up to 30,000 people each day come to look at my portrait.

Buried treasures

All rocks are made up of **minerals** — and some minerals can look very sparkly, if you polish them.

These four treasure maps show some of the best places in the world to dig up different kinds of minerals.

Remember: x marks the spot.

OPALS

Over 90% of all **opals** are from Australia. They have brilliant patterns that shimmer.

The most valuable kind of opals are black opals. They're found near the town of Lightning Ridge.

KYAWTHUITE

To search for the rarest type of mineral — **kyawthuite** — you should start digging in Myanmar.

 That's where the ONLY piece of kyawthuite has ever been found.

DIAMONDS

The largest ever polished **diamond** is this brown diamond. It's about the size of a lime.

GOLDEN JUBILEE DIAMOND

The diamond was removed from the ground in Cullinan, South Africa.

AFRICA

SOUTH AFRICA

Cullinan

EMERALDS

Much, much bigger than the Golden Jubilee Diamond is the largest **emerald** in the world.

BRAZIL

Bahia

SOUTH AMERICA

The Bahia Emerald is known after the state in Brazil where it was unearthed.

BAHIA EMERALD

It weighs more than a whole tiger.

Think how many rings you could make from this ONE emerald.

51

Around-the-world journeys

These adventurous people were the first to go around the planet in different ways. Below their pictures, you'll read how they got around, the year they finished and how long the journeys took.

Which of them did it fastest?

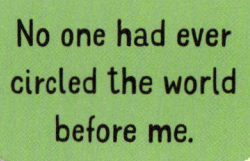

No one had ever circled the world before me.

 SAILING SHIP

 1522

 Two years, 50 weeks and three days

DAVE KUNST

I wore out 21 pairs of shoes with all that walking.

 ON FOOT

 1974

 Four years, 15 weeks and two days

RICK HANSEN

WHEELCHAIR

1987

Two years, eight weeks and six days

YURI GAGARIN

- SPACECRAFT
- 1961
- One hour and 48 minutes

JEANNE BARET

I was the first woman to go around the world.

- SAILING SHIP
- 1774
- About eight years

BERTRAND PICCARD & BRIAN JONES

- HOT-AIR BALLOON
- 1999
- 19 days, 21 hours and 55 minutes

JAMES GALLAGHER

- PLANE
- 1949
- Three days and 22 hours

Yuri Gagarin was FASTEST.

From outer space to the bottom of the ocean

The spot that's furthest away from any land on Earth is in the Pacific Ocean. Known as **Point Nemo**, it's home to more space junk than sharks.

There's so little to eat in the water that sea creatures rarely visit Point Nemo. It can be eerily quiet.

But there's a big SPLASH whenever parts of old spacecraft hit the surface.

Space scientists send them crashing down to this place because nobody lives anywhere nearby.

The junk sinks down to the ocean floor.

What on Earth is that?

Do aliens ever fly above Planet Earth and wonder what they're looking at? These are some of the alien's-eye views that they might see.

> Who drew the spider? It's bigger than a plane!

Around 2,000 years ago, people living near Nazca in Peru made all sorts of giant pictures, including this spider. They scraped away dark stones in lines to show the pale ground underneath.

When sunlight hits the ocean at a certain angle, it causes the surface to look spectacularly golden or silver. This is called sunglint.

> So shimmery!

Clouds can form, then vanish as they move over mountains. They make eye-catching patterns from above.

> Look at those zebra stripes in the sky.

Mirror, mirror on the ground

Welcome to **Salar de Uyuni** in Bolivia. There used to be a lake here. But it dried up thousands of years ago and left behind a thick crust of salt. This is called a **salt pan**.

Hardly any animals live here as there isn't much to eat.

But it's a useful place for flamingoes to take a break and rest their wings between long flights.

Is there anything below the salt?

I wonder what's underneath.

Brine power

If you were to chip away at the surface of Salar de Uyuni, you'd eventually uncover some very soggy mud. The mud is sopping wet with salty water called **brine**.

Look what we've found!

There's something rather special about this brine. It contains **lithium**, which is a soft type of metal.

The footprints that heat up the planet

Flying in planes, buying clothes, taking photos and all the other things that people do leave a **carbon footprint**. This means they are adding carbon dioxide and other gases to the air. These gases trap heat, which is why the planet is getting **warmer**.

POLAR BEAR

The gases are given off as things are made, used, transported and thrown away.

Our home in the Arctic is heating up faster than anywhere.

A hot planet is a problem for everyone. It causes both very dry and very wet weather, harming the places where people and animals live.

We know people can't stop leaving carbon footprints...

...BUT they can try to leave fewer of them by buying less and reusing more.

Super whales to the rescue!

As whales eat and grow bigger, they store huge amounts of carbon in their bodies. If the carbon wasn't inside them, it would become carbon dioxide in the air.

Whales have another superpower too — pooing...

MINKE WHALE

Saving the world, one poo at a time.

Whale poo mixes into seawater, helping tiny plant-like things called **phytoplankton** grow.

WHALE POO

PHYTOPLANKTON

Phytoplankton are incredibly useful for the planet. They take in carbon dioxide and give out **oxygen** that everyone needs to breathe.

All the **plants** in the world remove carbon dioxide from the air in the same way.

That's why it's important to plant lots more trees...

...and protect whales, too!

61

Glossary

Here you can find out the meanings of some of the words in this book...

algae — tiny plants that grow in water and inside **corals**

atmosphere — layers of different gases that surround Planet Earth

brine — salty water

capital — the main city in a country

continent — a very large area of land

corals — teams of sea creatures that build **reefs**

core — the extremely hot middle of Planet Earth

crater — a hole in the ground made by a **meteorite**

crops — plants that farmers grow for food

crust — the rocky outer layer of Planet Earth

desert — an extremely dry place where it very rarely rains

lava — hot, melted rock that sometimes rises out of the ground

mantle — the thickest layer inside Planet Earth

meteor — a space rock that burns up in the **atmosphere**

meteorite — a space rock that hits Planet Earth

meteoroid — a space rock outside the **atmosphere**

mineral — a solid thing that forms in the ground and makes up rocks

North Pole — the northernmost point on Planet Earth

oceanic trench — a deep crack in the seabed

rainforest — a lush, leafy forest where it rains a lot

reef — a raised part of the seabed, usually made by **corals**

South Pole — the southernmost point on Planet Earth

stalactite — a spine-shaped rock that hangs down inside caves

stalagmite — a spine-shaped rock that sticks up inside caves

volcano — a hill or mountain made when **lava** piles up

Index

Africa, 5, 40, 43, 51, 57
algae, 39, 62
Amazon Rainforest, 323
Amazon River, 23
Andes, 32
animals, 22, 23, 24, 25, 29, 31, 33, 38, 39, 40, 41, 42, 43, 47, 54, 58, 59, 60, 61
Antarctica, 5, 29
Arctic Ocean, 4
Asia, 5, 43, 50
Atlantic Ocean, 4
atmosphere, 36, 62
avocados, 27
aye-ayes, 43

bamboo, 22, 45
beaches, 12
bee hummingbirds, 43
Big Pineapple, the, 48
black pepper, 26
blue iguanas, 43
boats, 31, 37, 55
brine, 58, 59, 62
buildings, 45

cable cars, 31
capitals, 10, 62
carbon footprints, 60
carrots, 27
cave bacon, 35
cave popcorn, 35
caves, 34
cheese, 27

Chimborazo, 25
chocolate, 27
cities, 10, 13, 16, 19, 31
clouds, 56
coast redwoods, 22
cocoa, 27
continents, 2, 4, 18, 19, 62
corals, 38, 39, 62
core, 9, 62
countries, 10, 16, 17, 20
craters, 37, 62
crops, 26, 62
crust, 8, 62

dates, 26
deserts, 12, 32, 40-41, 62
diamonds, 51
Dyrehavsbakken, 49

earthquakes, 45
emeralds, 51
Equator, the, 25
Europe, 5

farms, 13, 26, 27, 28
fennec foxes, 40, 41
flags, 16
flamingoes, 58
food, 26-27, 33
forests, 13, 22-23

Galápagos giant tortoises, 42
Gibraltar campions, 32

globes, 3, 18
Great Pyramid of Giza, the, 49

hippos, 31

ice, 13, 18, 19, 29
Indian Ocean, 4
internet, the, 55
islands, 42-43, 57

kangaroo paws, 33
kyawthuite, 501

lakes, 12, 13, 37, 58
languages, 20-21
lava, 44, 62
lithium, 58, 59
Louvre, the, 49

mantle, 8, 62
Mariana Trench, the, 46-47
Mauna Kea, 24, 25
metals, 9, 58, 59
meteorites, 37, 62
meteoroids, 36, 37, 62
meteors, 36, 62
minerals, 50-51, 62
Moon, the, 14
Mount Everest, 24, 25

mountains, 13, 24-25, 32, 48, 56

national anthems, 17
Niesen mountain, 49
night, 3, 14, 15, 19, 36
North America, 5, 22, 43
North Pole, the, 14, 62
Northern Lights, the, 14

ocean floor, 24, 54, 55
Oceania, 5, 50
oceanic trenches, 46, 62
oceans, 4, 8, 12, 13, 19
olive oil, 26
opals, 50
oranges, 27

Pacific Ocean, 4, 46, 54
penguins, 29
people, 6-7, 20, 21, 27, 52, 53
plants, 13, 22, 28, 32-33, 39, 57, 61
Point Nemo, 54
polyps, 38, 39

pygmy sloths, 43

quinoa, 26

rain, 23, 28, 34, 37, 41, 59
rainforests, 23, 62
reefs, 38-39, 62
rice, 28
Rideau Canal, 48
River Nile, 57
rivers, 12, 13, 23, 31, 57
rocks, 8, 34, 35, 36, 44, 50

saguaros, 32
Sahara, 40
Salar de Uyuni, 58-59
salt pans, 58, 59
sand, 12, 40, 41
soda straws, 35
Sonoran Desert, 32
South America, 5, 42, 51
South Pole, the, 15, 62
Southern Lights, the, 15
Southern Ocean, 4

space, 3, 25, 36, 54, 56, 57
stalactites, 34, 62
stalagmites, 34, 62
stars, 14
Statue of Liberty, the, 48
Statue of Unity, the, 48
streams, 33
summer, 15
Sun, the, 3, 14, 39, 40, 41, 46, 56

tamaraws, 43
titan arums, 33
trains, 31

vanilla, 27
volcanoes, 44, 62

wasabi, 33
whales, 61
winter, 14, 15

yaretas, 32

Additional design by Helena Towell and Katie Webb

Series editor: Ruth Brocklehurst
Series designer: Helen Lee

First published in 2026 by Usborne Publishing Limited, 83-85 Saffron Hill, London EC1N 8RT, United Kingdom. usborne.com Copyright © 2026 Usborne Publishing Limited. The name Usborne and the Balloon logo are registered trade marks of Usborne Publishing Limited. All rights reserved. No part of this publication may be reproduced or used in any manner for the purpose of training artificial intelligence technologies or systems (including for text or data mining), stored in retrieval systems or transmitted in any form or by any means without prior permission of the publisher. UKE.

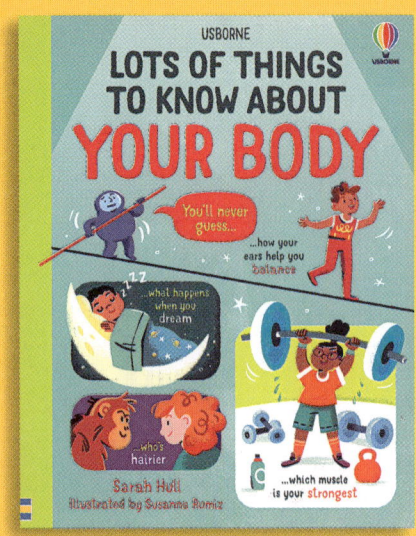
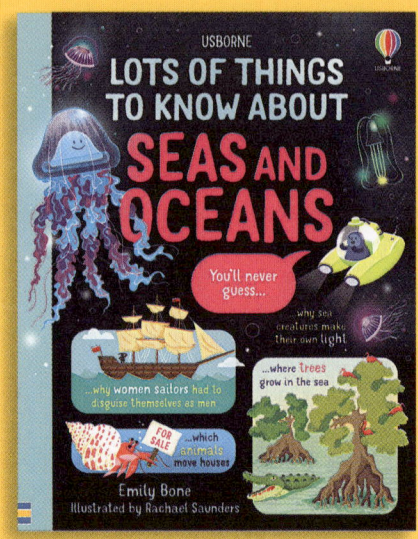